Chinese Modern Engineering

BRIDGES

Edited by Xia Rui

Written by Zou Jiahui

Illustrated by Wang Futing

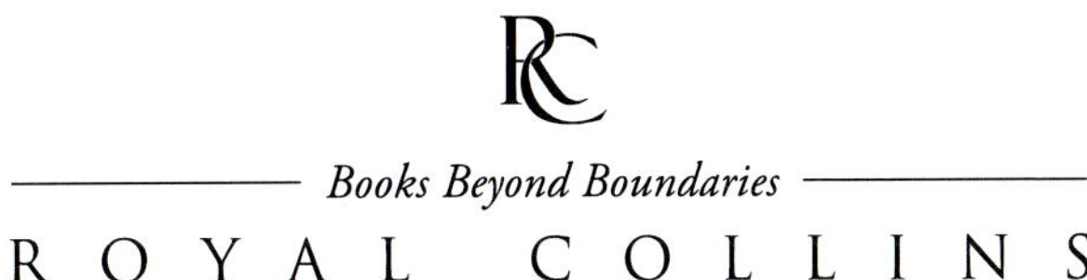

Books Beyond Boundaries

ROYAL COLLINS

Hong Kong-Zhuhai-Macau Bridge

This is the longest sea-crossing bridge in the world. *The Guardian* praises it as one of the Seven Modern Wonders of the World. This 55-km-bridge, containing the world's longest undersea immersed pipe tunnel, connects Hong Kong on the east and Zhuhai and Macau on the west and reduces the land travel time among the three places from four hours to 30 minutes.

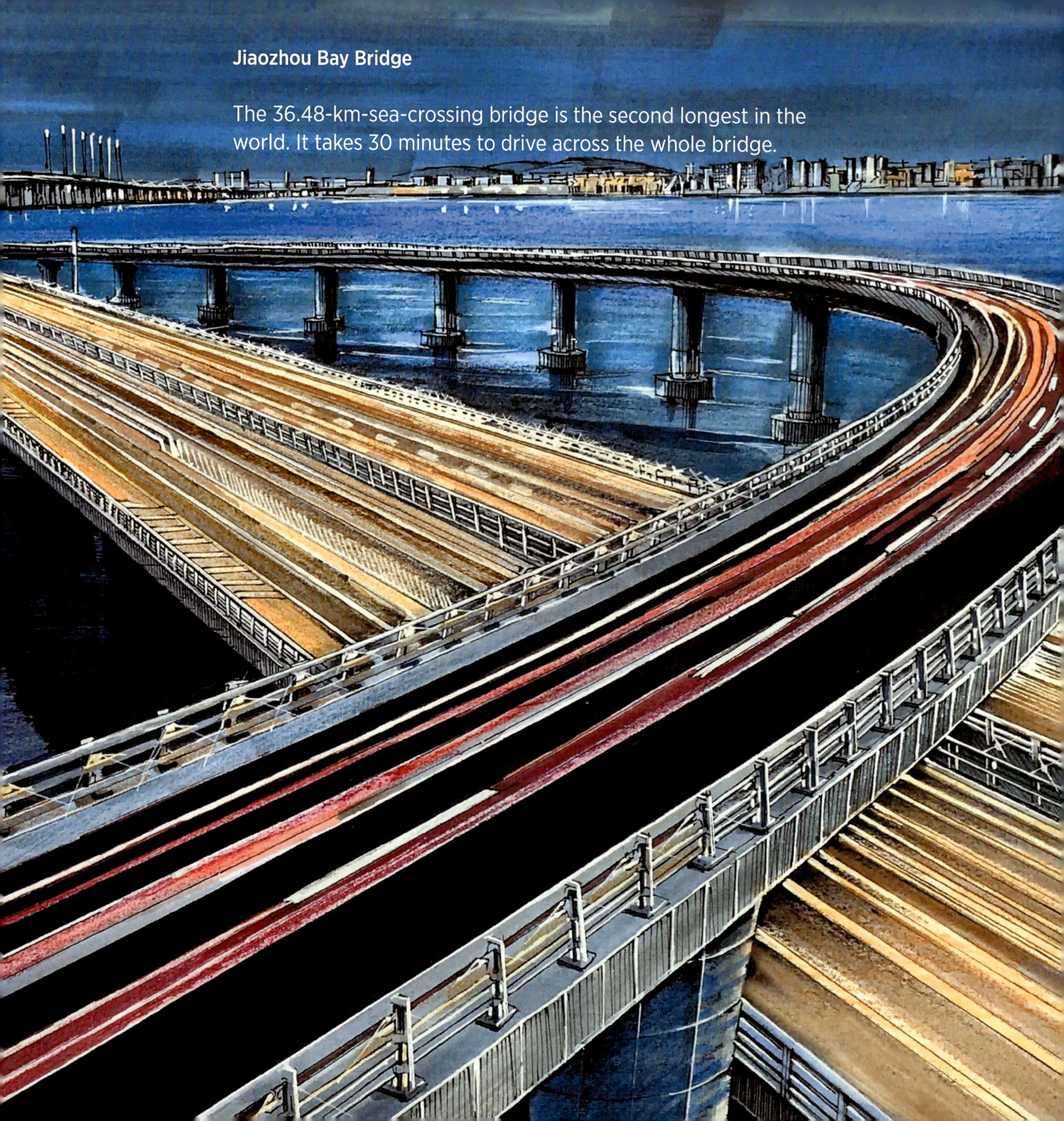

Jiaozhou Bay Bridge

The 36.48-km-sea-crossing bridge is the second longest in the world. It takes 30 minutes to drive across the whole bridge.

Hangzhou Bay Bridge

It is 480 meters shorter than Jiaozhou Bay Bridge, which is approximately the length of one lap round the outer circle of the sports field. The guardrails are in seven colors that change every 5 km. The bridge is S-shaped with few straight-lines of any distance. This can make drivers less tired when driving.

In addition to crossing seas, bridges can cross big rivers and valleys as well.

The Nanjing Yangtze River Bridge is China's first self-designed and self-made double deck railway and highway bridge. After it was finished, the Nanjing Yangtze River Bridge was recorded in *The Guinness World Records,* as "the world's longest highway and railway bridge." While it took 1.5 hours for the train to cross the river by ferry in the past, it now only takes two minutes.

The Changyuan-Dongming Yellow River Bridge is 33,733 feet long. It is part of the Xinxiang-Heze railway and a super bridge across the Yellow River, connecting Changyuan County in Henan Province and Dongming County in Shandong Province. It is titled "the longest railway bridge in Asia."

The Sidu River Bridge was built at the boundary of Yichang and Enshi in Hubei Province, and this bridge is the world's longest suspension bridge in a deep mountain canyon. The height difference between the top of the bridge tower to the bottom of the canyon is 2,133 feet. The bridge deck is 1,837 feet above the bottom of the canyon, which is the height of a 200-story building.

The Beipanjiang Bridge (Duge Bridge) is the world's highest bridge. It is located between Yunnan and Guizhou Provinces above the Beipanjiang Canyon. The height difference between the bridge deck and the bottom of the canyon is 1,854 feet.

Based on their building types, bridges can be divided into arch bridges, beam bridges, cable-stayed bridges, and suspension bridges.

An arch bridge has an upward bending surface, like a rainbow.

The Seventeen Hole Bridge is the largest stone bridge in the Summer Palace in Beijing. The bridge is 492 feet long with seventeen archways below. On the guardrails, there are 544 stone lions in different sizes and shapes.

A Beam Bridge is the oldest and the most common bridge type in China. In the past, people called it a flat bridge. Its structure and shape are simple, and it can be easily built just by erecting wood or slate on both banks of a valley or river.

The Pazhou Bridge is an 11,811-foot-long bridge in Guangzhou that crosses the Zhu River.

A cable-stayed bridge depends on cables and the bridge towers to pull the main beam upward. These are the three main elements of a cable-stayed bridge.

The Stonecutters' Bridge is a 1.6-km-bridge in Hong Kong and is a world-famous cable-stayed bridge.

A suspension bridge has steel cables on cable towers to sustain the bridge deck.

The Runyang Yangtze River Bridge connects Zhenjiang and Yangzhou in Jiangsu Province. The south bridge is a suspension bridge of 4,888 feet long. It is one of the ten longest suspension bridges in the world.

Chaotianmen Bridge

Chinese bridges are famous worldwide, with six of the ten longest concrete filled steel tubular arch bridges with the largest single span length. Number one is the **Chaotianmen Bridge in Chongqing**. Number two is the **Lupu Bridge in Shanghai**.

Lupu Bridge in Shanghai

China has seven out of the ten longest cable-stayed bridges in the world. Number three is **Suzhou-Nantong Yangtze River Bridge** in Jiangsu Province. China has five out of the ten longest suspension bridges.

Another example is the **Xihoumen Bridge** on the Zhoushan Archipelago, in Zhejiang Province.

Today, sea-crossing and canyon-crossing bridges have very long spans and great heights. Their building materials have also changed from wood and stone to steel and reinforced concrete. These pose higher demands for bridge construction.

Many innovative endeavors have been carried out in the aspects of windproofing, quakeproofing, and anti-corrosion in order to make bridges more sustainable.

Modern sea-crossing bridges are made of marine durable concrete and anti-corrosion steel. Important parts will be covered by an anti-corrosion coating, a steel corrosion inhibitor, and additional current cathodic protection will be applied to prevent bridges from corroding.

Anti-corrosion coating

Windbreaks can effectively slow down wind flow and ensure safe driving.

Viscous fluid damper is like a “safety airbag” for bridges. It can reduce the impact of an earthquake on the building structure to the greatest extent and alleviate the consequential damage.

Marine durable concrete

Anti-corrosion steel

In ancient times, Chinese engineers had already mastered high-level bridge building techniques.

The Zhaozhou Bridge, which was built in the Sui Dynasty (6th–7th century A.D.), is over 1,400 years old. It is the oldest and most well-preserved stone arch bridge in the world.

The Zhaozhou Bridge is also called the Anji Bridge. It is located in Zhao County, in Hebei Province. It spans across the 121-foot-wide Jiao River and is made completely of stones. Local people call it "Big Stone Bridge."

Lugou Bridge is the oldest stone multi-arch bridge preserved in Beijing. There are 501 stone lions in different shapes and postures on the guardrails. The bigger ones are as tall as children, and the smaller ones are only the size of a fist.

The Luoyang Bridge in Fujian Province was historically called the Wan'an Bridge. Built in the Northern Song Period (10th–12th century A.D.), it is the oldest sea-crossing stone beam bridge preserved in China. In order to protect the bridge pier at that time, people raised oysters on the stone pillars.

The Guangji Bridge in Guangdong is a very special example of an ancient Chinese bridge that integrates a beam bridge, a pontoon bridge, and an arch bridge. It has 18 boats and 24 piers. It is acknowledged as one of the four ancient bridges in China, along with Zhaozhou Bridge, Luoyang Bridge, and Lugou Bridge.

Why do people build bridges?

The idea of humans overpowering and changing nature has always been deeply ingrained in Chinese traditional culture. So, the Chinese people never retreat when they come across mountains or rivers; instead, they build roads, bridges, and channels to help them through.

Today, more bridges are being built in China. For example, the country is planning to build a sea-crossing bridge that connects Guangdong and Hainan provinces on the two sides of the **Qiongzhou Strait**, the “golden waterway” and one of the three straits of China.

It now takes about five hours to cross the **Qiongzhou Strait** by ferry (waiting time and travelling time combined). But when the bridge is finished, it will only take 30 minutes to cross the strait by car.

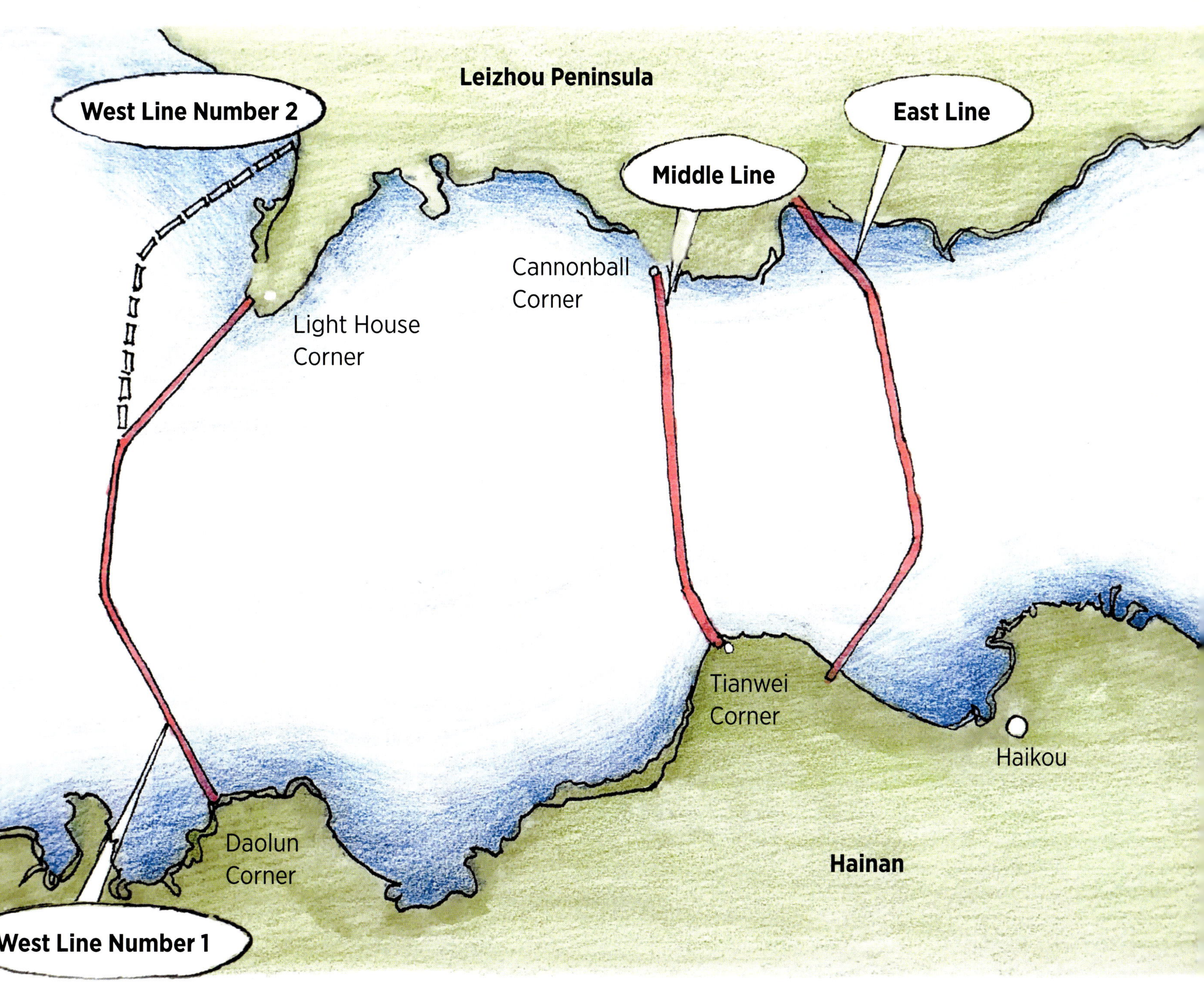

ABOUT THE EDITOR:

Xia Rui is the general manager of the Jiangsu Qiaomu Education Technology Co., Ltd. He graduated from the Department of Chemistry in the National University of Singapore, and then started teaching Cambridge and Oxford University Entrance courses in the International Department of the Nanjing Foreign Languages School. He is proficient in English, physics, chemistry, mathematics, and other disciplines. He has written and directed many books, such as *Exam Key Points Analysis*, *Calculation Expert*, and *Preparatory Courses*, which are considered first-line brands in the market.

ABOUT THE ILLUSTRATOR:

Wang Futing graduated from the School of Animation in the China Academy of Art. Her graduation works have won the Silver Award in the Taiwan Creative Design Competition, the Bronze Award of the Kunshan Animation Fest, and the Finalist Award of China International Animation Fest. Ever since her graduation, Wang has worked as a professional illustrator for picture books and commercials. She participated in the R&D and illustration project for the *Modern Engineering* picture book series.

CHINESE MODERN ENGINEERING:
BRIDGES

Edited by Xia Rui
Written by Zou Jiahui
Illustrated by Wang Futing

First published in 2022 by Royal Collins Publishing Group Inc.
Groupe Publication Royal Collins Inc.
BKM Royalcollins Publishers Private Limited

Headquarters: 550-555 boul. René-Lévesque O Montréal (Québec) H2Z1B1 Canada
India office: 805 Hemkunt House, 8th Floor, Rajendra Place, New Delhi 110 008

ISBN: 978-1-4878-0942-3

To find out more about our publications, please visit www.royalcollins.com.